MORE MONOLOGUES FOR TEENAGERS

Roger Karshner

Dramaline® Publications

Dramaline Publications
36-851 Palm View Road
Rancho Mirage, CA 92270
Phone 760/770-6076 Fax 760/770-4507
E-Mail: dramaline@aol.com Web: www.dramaline.com

Library of Congress Cataloging-in-Publication Data

Karshner, Roger.
　　More Monologues for Teenagers/Roger Karshner
p. cm.
ISBN 0-949669-44-7 (alk.paper)
1. Monologues. 2. Teenagers Drama. I. Title.
PN2080 .K318 1999
812'.54—dc21　　　　　　　　　　　　　　99-32513

Cover Design by John Sabel

This book is printed on acid-free paper, a paper that meets the requirements of the American Standard of Permanence of paper for printed library material.

CONTENTS

YOUNG WOMEN

JILLIAN

Jillian, a student in a small-town high school, has a brother who is gay. Here, she tells of his struggles with his sexuality, his self-outing, and the subsequent problems generated by it both at home and on campus. A loving sister, she defends him while admonishing those whose narrow-mindedness and ridicule have inflicted great pain.

My brother, Danny, always seemed just like everybody else. I mean, he played sports and dated and everything, just like the other boys. There was never any indication that he was gay. Not until last fall. This is when, unexpectedly, he came out.

He told us—my mom and dad and me—one night while we were having dinner. Wow! It was, like, this bombshell, you know. My mom was pretty cool, but my dad went totally crazy, flew into this violent rage. I thought for a moment he was going to beat Dan up. He said stuff like being gay was sick and against God and perverted. It was just awful. Mom had to calm him down.

Dan's been openly gay now for about six months and it's really turned his life around. Sometimes I wonder if he wouldn't have been better off not saying anything and just moving away after he graduated; this way he could have avoided the hurt and all of the stupid comments.

He faces constant abuse and humiliation at school. People are always whispering behind his back and calling him "faggot" under their breath. And one day, while we were walking home from school, these guys from this punk-metal band surrounded us and starting calling Dan a faggot and threatened to kick his butt. One of these totally stupid fools even shoved Danny, which was a big mistake, because Danny is super-strong and he threw the jerk aside like a bag of garbage—which he was.

Danny hangs with other gays who've formed this group for the better understanding of homosexuality. It's really a nice bunch of kids and there's a lot of love between them. But they get ripped by the totally ignorant locals. Even our two-bit newspaper has run stuff against them. And you should read the hate letters to the editor.

At least my dad has come around. In fact, when he heard about those creeps hassling Danny, it was all we could do to keep him from wasting them.

You know what? Dan's no different than he ever was. He's still kind and considerate and his being gay doesn't have anything to do with anything. And after all, he's a human being, and more than that, he's my brother.

4

ELLEN

An attack of serious jealously nearly resulted in the breakup of a long-term relationship. Here, Ellen discusses the problem and tells what she has learned from her mistakes.

Looking back on it, the whole thing was totally ridiculous. The way I behaved was childish and embarrassing.

Jeremy and I had been going together since the 10th grade— really steady. We were together all the time, and when we weren't, we were talking on the phone. We were this close. *(holds up her index and forefinger)* Really tight. Then, because Jeremy's grades were slipping, his parents decided that we shouldn't see each other so much. So, we only got to hang out on weekends. In the meantime, Jeremy hooks up with this super-brain, Charlotte Walker, who is helping him with his studies, okay? Walker is the school know-it-all whose IQ is almost as big as her boobs, which were a much bigger threat to me than her smarts.

The reason I got jealous was because it seemed he could always find time to do stuff with her, but he didn't have time for me. I got the leftovers for a few hours on Sunday. I totally freaked.

I made up my mind right then and there that I wasn't going to be one-upped by some big-boobed brain who talked like an encyclopedia. No way. So I decided to bone up on literature and poetry and stuff so I could impress Jeremy when we were together I figured if Jeremy dug high-IQ types, I'd get into Shakespeare and some of the other heavy-duty literature guys. I figured I could match Walker in the smarts department. In the boobs department . . . well, that's another story. You can

5

memorize a sonnet, but you can't pull a D-cup out of a book. No way I was going to beat her back-to-nature boobs.

Anyway, I crammed on some Molière and Ibsen and the next Sunday I laid some cool lines from *A Doll's House* on him. Know what? My plan fell totally flat. He didn't show any reaction at all. Man, was it ever a drag. Made me feel more invisible than ever.

Then I realized what I was doing. I thought to myself: This is really stupid. This isn't me. What am I doing here?

So I decided to back off and just be me and to have an honest talk with Jeremy about how I felt. It was the coolest thing I could have done. Now I'm not jealous because I realize that Jeremy's interest in Walker is not boob-oriented. It's strictly academic. And the smart-ass *is* helping him. He got an A in English last semester.

And I got a Master's Degree in growing up.

LAURA

Laura tells her girlfriend she's had it with dating immature, unsophisticated high-school guys.

Forget it! No way! No way I'm going out with Harry Simons or any other boys my age. I'd rather stay home and watch reruns. In fact, I'm sick and tired of going out with these cheesy jerks; guys whose idea of a big evening is a bad movie and a Coke. And they always pick the movie, too; some action-adventure flick with guys running around blowing each other away and a soundtrack like a car wreck. Then for the price of the ticket and the watered down cola, they wanna grope and squeeze you like your ripe fruit. Forget it. (*beat.*)

Whose cute? Harry Simons? He's about a cute as acne. And his breath is lethal. He must brush with dog poop. C'mon, he's just another unsophisticated idiot. They all are. Lemme ask you, when was the last time you had a really cool date? (*beat*)

With Jim Harper? You gotta be kidding! You told me he showed up at the movie with his own popcorn. (*beat.*)

But he was nice. So what? I don't care how nice he is, he's gotta be a total penny-pinching jerk to show up with his own popcorn. Weren't you totally embarrassed? Someone like that probably wears used underwear. Yuck! Where'd he take you afterward? To his house for leftover chicken?

It's the same with all of them, I'm telling you. They're all cheap and stupid and totally rude. None of them know how to treat a woman. Can you imagine your dad ever treating your mom like this? Hey, people were cool back in the old days. Men were gentlemen who treated women with respect. They knew how to move, they had manners. You know what? My dad still opens the car door for my mom. (*beat*) Yours, too? Well . . .

7

there you are. See. This is what I'm talking about. When's the last time someone opened the car door for you? (*beat*) You can't remember, right? The answer is *nev-er*. You kidding? They'd drive off and leave you standing in the rain before they'd walk around.

That's it. I've had it. No more dates with cheap, rude, young jerks. I don't need it. I can wait, okay? (*beat*) Who? Mark Chapman? Oh, you mean that cute new guy from Canada. What about him? (*beat*) He did? (*beat*) He didn't? He actually said that? About me? (*preening, flattered*) No kidding? Wow! Maybe he'll ask me out. (*beat*) Huh? I said I wasn't going out with any more boys my age. Well . . . yeah . . . right . . . right. But you gotta be open-minded, you know. You have to make exceptions.

LINDSAY

She just can't fathom some people's fixation with death.

What is it with these people who love funerals? It's like they just can't get enough of the dead. They just love visitations. "Don't mind me, I'm just hanging around enjoying the body." In fact, I think they like dead people better than live people. And . . . well . . . come to think of it, there *are* advantages, I guess. I mean, like, dead people don't talk back, they're quiet, respectful, they don't interrupt, they don't lie, they don't steal, they're clean, they're always dressed nice, they never show up at your house unexpectedly when you're sitting around trimming your toenails. Hey, in some ways, I guess they're perfect.

What is it with their hands always being folded over their chests? What if they'd been in the military? Wouldn't it be more realistic if they were saluting? (*salutes*) Or if they'd been politicians? (*waves*) Or impatient drivers . . . ? *(gives "the finger")*.

Have you ever noticed how people talk to the corpse? Weird. Far out. They say stuff like, "Well, take it easy now, Jane." How easy can you take it? If dead isn't easy, I don't wanna go. Or, "Well, now you'll be with your friends." What if they didn't have any friends? Like my uncle, Leonard, who was universally hated by everybody. Of course, when he died he wa, "a wonderful person." "Wouldn't hurt a fly." "Everybody loved him." "He'll be missed." How could he be missed? Nobody would have anything to do with him. But now that he's dead, he was sweet, wonderful, kind, and generous. Generous. I guess alluva sudden everyone forgets about the time he got caught taking money out of a March of Dimes display. But now he's

9

dead, so now he's perfect, now he's going to join Aunt Rose, who divorced him for exposing himself to her Meals on Wheels woman.

Then there are the remarks about how good the body looks. "Doesn't he look good?" "Isn't she beautiful?" "She never looked lovlier." When you're alive, all you hear is how rotten you look. "You don't look so good." "Have you been getting enough sleep?" "If I were you, and I don't mean to alarm you, I'd see a doctor." When you're alive, nobody ever tells you how good you look. But die and it's, "Doesn't he look good?" "Isn't she beautiful?" Why is it you have to die before you get compliments?

DIANE

Diane, obviously a keen observer of the human condition, remarks on some of its contrasts and contradictions.

You ever notice when people are big how they like things that are little? You weigh 300 pounds, what do you do? You go out and buy a little car. You go out and buy a Miata even though once you get in it you can't close the door. You rent a little apartment and sleep in a little bed and shop at a mini-mart. And you buy clothes that are too small. You buy little pants and little dresses. You cram your butt into little Levi's. Let me ask you . . . . does the end justify the jeans? And you buy little shoes. You wear a 9EEE, you break the laces trying on 7As. But you buy them and wear them anyway, even though you walk around like a penguin. But that's okay—they're little. Little is okay, little is good, little is acceptable.

And big fat people walk little. (*walks mincy*). Like they're barefoot walking through a field of worms. (*mimes this*). Oh, God! I think I just scrunched a nightcrawler. But big fat people are good dancers and swimmers and they're always happy. Right? How do we know this? We hang around ballrooms watching for fat dancers? We go to the beach on the lookout for fat swimmers? How many happy fat people do you know? None. How can you be happy with all those chins? It'd be like playing an accordion with your neck. (*shudders*). I don't know about you, but I don't think big fat people can be happy. Obesity is yuck, not yocks. And did you ever notice how these big fat people have a thing for little people. You see a fat man, you see him with a woman his size? No way. You see him with a pigmy. You see a fat woman you see her with a guy who looks like a string of beef jerky.

11

And why are these little people with big fat people in the first place? Because little people like things that are *big*. Little people are big into big. You ever notice how they wear big clothes and drive big cars? How they live in big houses and eat big meals? They talk big, walk big, and ram their cart into you at the supermarket. "I'm skinny, I'm a dwarf, look out I'm coming through." My aunt Ida was four feet tall, weighed 80 pounds. She drove a Lincoln Town Car, lived in a mansion, and ate a roast every morning for breakfast. She had big furniture and a walk-in freezer and a king-sized bed. She had a big-screen TV. She always bought the giant economy size. She was totally hungup on big. She visited the Grand Canyon and couldn't even remember that it was in Arizona, all she could remember was that it was big. "God, it was big," she said.

When she died she was laid out in a big casket, which made her look like a blanched peanut. If you filed by too fast you missed her altogether.

Are people ever totally weird, or what?

ESTHER

Esther has become impatient with the inanity of everyday circumstances. Here, in her "stupid" speech, she cites examples.

You go to a restaurant, like, just two of you, okay? And what does the maitre d' ask? "How many?" How many could it be? Here you are, two of you, the only two people within fifty feet, but he asks, "How many?" And why does he do this? Because he's stupid. If he weren't stupid, he'd said say, "Right this way," not, "How many?" Now, if he doesn't ask, "How many?" what does he ask? He asks, "How many in your party?" Alluva sudden two of you have become a party and you're not even wearing funny hats. Why? Because he's stupid.

You're standing at the counter with a toaster and the salesperson comes up and asks, "Can I help you?" What does he think he can do? I mean . . .you're there, right? You have a toaster on the counter, right? Still he asks, "Can I help you?" No, you don't need help, you just came in to brown up some rye bread. Then he asks, "Can I show you something in a toaster." You'd like to say, "Yes, your head," but you don't, because you're trying to be civil, which isn't easy because you're talking with a stupid person. Then, when you hand him your credit card and he asks, "Will this be cash or charge?" you say, "Charge," because by now you're just as stupid as he is.

Did you ever wonder why the bank gives you ATM privileges when half the time the machine's out of money? It's late at night, you don't have a dime, you're low on gas, and the machine tells you, "Sorry. Temporarily out of money." Which means, they're out of *your* money. This means you're alluva sudden broke because your bank is temporarily out of business.

13

And it's not even their money! It's money you deposited because one of the advantages they offered you was an ATM card so you could get your money. But now they're out of money, which means they ran out of *your* money before you got there, which means somebody else got to your money first. Somebody else is running around with your money.

When you ask, "What's the point of issuing an ATM card in the first place?" they reply, "Because it's a convenience." Which means, even with over two billion in assets, they're stupid.

AUDRY

Things often aren't as advertised.

Do real estate people really sell real estate? Or do they just show up and struggle with the lock box while you're standing back getting rained on? What do these people do all day other than sit around dreaming up stuff that makes rubble sound good?

My mom sees this ad in the paper: Spacious, lovely, three-bedroom, three-bath charmer in an ideal location. Formal dining room. Room for den or office. Newly remodeled kitchen. Situated on a heavenly one-quarter-acre lot with abounding views. Near transportation. Owner motivated. $200,000. Sam Gordon, Green Hills Properties.

Okay, so she called Green Hills and asked for Sam Gordon. The receptionist says, "Mr. Gordon is on caravan." So she left her name and number. That night, during dinner, Sam Gordon calls back and says, "I hope I'm not interrupting your dinner," even though Mom's mouth was full of pizza. "And here is a guy who want's to sell us a $200,000 house. Anyway, she arranged for him to show us the place the next morning.

When we arrive, the neighborhood is not an "ideal location." Next door, an old car was up on blocks in the driveway, and across the street two refugees from *Deliverance* are sitting on an old couch gnawing chicken legs. We nodded and they smiled, and even from three-hundred feet you could see that their teeth were greener than Ireland.

Finally, after twenty minutes, Sam Gordon rolls up. He says, "Beautiful morning." Yeah, "beautiful" all right. Beautiful if it wasn't drizzling and cold and people from Briar Patch weren't throwing chicken bones into their front lawn.

Sam Gordon points out the "abounding views," which are of the rusted-out car, the two geeks, and a vacant lot full of discarded Hefty bags full of crap. When Mom asks him if this is where they dump the dismembered bodies, he says, "Certainly not," either because he has no sense of humor or because he knows where the dismembered bodies *are* dumped. Either way, this didn't exactly instill buyer confidence.

Inside, the place isn't a "charmer," it's an alarmer. And, as he shows us around, Sam Gordon says, "Here you have your living room. Here you have your kitchen. Here you have your bedroom. Here you have your dining area. Here you have your built-in range."

After a half-hour of "here you haves," he's shocked when Mom tells him the house doesn't live up to the ad copy. When she laughingly suggested it was written by Omar Khyyam, he discreetly said his office didn't hire Arabs. This does it.

We've decided to stay in our apartment. Even though we can hear the woman upstairs scream at her husband, we figure we're better off renting.

BRITTANY

Brittany has found that giving her time, involving herslef in a positive cause, has been an uplifting,, positive experience.

At first, when my teacher approached me, I was, like, forget it. Like I have enough stuff to handle with my studies and my responsibilities at home and looking after my kid bother, who's, like, this little annoying creep. So when she asked me if I wanted to get involved with pre-school and elementary kids at the YMCA I took a pass.

Then, when my girlfriend, Sharon, and my steady, Jim, got in to the program, well . . . my attitude changed. They were so stoked on what they were doing I couldn't help but be kinda curious. They said that it was one of the coolest things they've ever done. So I got hooked up with the program last fall.

What we do is get involved with kids at lower levels. It's called the Teen Teaching Program. What we do is help kids with their studies, help them improve their grades and skills and the like, and develop an understanding and appreciation for the importance of education and community involvement. We not only work with them on their studies, we also promote the idea of being good citizens and involving themselves in community services when they're older. What we're hoping to achieve is this circular effect that will go on and on from one generation to the other.

I had this one girl, Jamie, who was really tough to deal with. Even though she was super-sharp, she was sullen and indifferent and had a smart-ass mouth. I don't know why she was in the program. She challenged everything I said to the point I wanted to belt her. One day I finally said, "Hey, look, garbage mouth, if you don't want to listen, you're outta here."

17

Know what? She started to cry. Wow! I felt awful. Turns out her home life was a mess and that her stepdad put her down all the time, gave her credit for nothing. Her self-esteem was zero. This was the reason she lashed out at everyone. She begged me not to kick her out of the program, said she would catch hell at home. It was pitiful to see how frightened she was. So I told her everything was cool, no problem. All I asked was for her cooperation.

Since then, Jamie is a different person. I guess all she needed was a second chance and understanding. Something she never got at home. I learned a lot from this. Even though I was the teacher, I learned an important lesson, which is you have to get under people's skin, understand where they're coming from before you start making judgments.

Jamie's fine now. One of our counselors talked with her family and things are better between her and her stepdad.

The program has done a lot for me. Helping others has helped me grow up. I'm more mellow now. My brother's not even an annoying creep anymore. Most of the time.

CINDY

Cindy reads the riot act to her mother's live-in boyfriend.

You're not my father, so shut up! (*beat*) Oh, yeah? Well, I'm not taking any crap from you, okay? You move in here like some big damned deal and try to take over and run everything and boss people around. Well, you're not bossing me. (*beat*) Oh, is that right? Well, in the first place, I don't believe my mother ever said that. And in the second place, if she did, I'm still not going to be ordered around in my own home by some loser. (*beat*) Yeah, loser!

Look at you, sitting around in your robe at eleven o'clock in the morning staring at the sports page while my mom's out working. Don't you have any pride? (*beat*) Well, I'm not your daughter, and don't ever forget it. And, if I were, I'd be totally embarrassed to admit it because you're such a nothing, lazy lowlife. Look, you may have Mom fooled, but not me, mister. (*beat*) Oh, yeah? And just what are you going to do about it? You ever raise a hand to me and I'll tell my father and he'll chop you up in little pieces.

No wonder kids never want to get married anymore. Not when they see what their parents put each other through and how they behave—like children, like two-year-olds. Like Mom moving you in here. She must have been out of her mind. (*beat*) Oh, so I'm just a spoiled brat, huh? Because I won't take any crap from you I'm a spoiled brat. Well, at least I'm not a damned leech, a no-good, lazy bastard who's too good for honest work. (*beat*) Don't threaten me, you jerk!

I've told my dad about you, and he's plenty mad, so don't go pressing your luck around here, okay? If I ever told him how you sit around here in front of TV all day sucking up beer, he'd

19

run your loser butt out of here fast, don't think he wouldn't. You'd be history in a minute. So watch what you say.

I'm on to you, mister big phony; on to your lies and kissing up to my mother because she's a meal ticket. And I'm also on to the hang-up phone calls every day at the same time. You think I don't know what that's all about, with you leaving smelling like a cologne factory right after? (*beat*) What? You think I'm buying that, that you're playing golf? C'mon. I'd laugh if I wouldn't puke. You think I'm some kind of idiot here? What about the lipstick I found on your golf shirt? (*beat*) I took it out of your car trunk. (*beat*) Oh, so I'm a prying little trouble-maker, huh? You bet I am. And I intend to be *big* trouble because I'm showing her the shirt tonight. Oh, I wouldn't, would I? Hey, you didn't get that on the golf course, creep. Not unless you've got some kind of strange caddie.

It's been rotten knowing you, loser! (*turns and makes a quick exit*)

RONI

The scene: an upscale clothing store. Even though her outfit's cool, she's afraid it would be rejected by her mother. While observing herself in a tri-plex mirror, she comments to her bud Cindy.

This is really cool, but I could never take it home. (*beat*) Are you kidding? My mother would kill me. (*beat*) C'mon, Cindy, your mom's a different story, she's cool, she into what's happening. My mother's strictly yesterday's papers—sensible shoes, tight little perms, *Woman's Day,* and oatmeal cookies. She's lava lamps and the "Jetsons". You don't know how lucky you are, Cin. To have a mom like yours, I mean. (*turning before the mirror*) Your mom's, like, living in the present, she's today, uptown, on top of stuff.

She'd never go for the purple thing, not in a million years. (*beat*) No way. Her favorite color is stark white. I may as well forget it. How she's gonna go for something like this when she still hassles me about having my ears pierced? (*observing herself) favorably*) Is this totally cool, or what? And it fits really good, too. And I *love* the shoes. The platforms make me three inches taller. But she'd freak. She thinks we all should be wearing Bass Weegans. (*beat*) Oh yeah? You have no idea. how conservative she is.

Remember that blue camouflage skirt I bought? The tight one with the neat slit? Well, she took a trip to outerspace over that one. (*beat*) Oh yeah. She went nuts. You'd think I'd brought home a rattlesnake, or something. Totally freaked, said I looked like a streetwalker. Even asked me if I was doing drugs and hanging out with gangs. You haven't got any idea what I'm living with, Cin. Where your mom's hip and understanding and keeps up with the times, mine's a total retard about anything modern. You've seen the way she dresses. She looks like a Pilgrim, or something. You'd think it would turn off my dad. Maybe it does. Maybe this is the reason he's always on the road and works late at the office. I mean, after all, who want's to be married to Betsy Ross?

I guess I could maybe sneak it into the house; take it out in my backpack and put it on at school. Naw, she'd catch it on the credit card bill. And I don't have enough cash. What's cash?

I guess I'll just have to keep dressing like a peasant till I go to college.

ADRIANNA

They say all's fair in love and war. Well, due to her parent's bitter divorce proceedings, Adrianna has the impression that perhaps love and war are one and the same.

Whadya do? You do your best. You try not to get in between and take sides. You try to be fair and impartial. But it doesn't work because they're both off-the-wall crazy and full of hate over furniture, cars, and money—mostly money. Money calls the tune when people decide to split.

At first, when my dad and mom decided to separate, everything was like, I don't want anything, everything's cool, we have to be civilized. Everything was like, We really still like each other and don't want any big hassle or scenes, all we want is our freedom, we'll always be good friends.

Like this was before my mom sued for divorce and asked for everything, including stuff like dishes and plates and nickel-and-dime crap that alluva sudden became real valuable. Asking for the house and cars and stuff was one thing, but when she asked for the money and CDs and stocks and bonds and stuff, it hit the fan. Alluva sudden my dad's calling up screaming and she's screaming back what a no-good creep he is and how he left her for a younger woman and how all he ever thinks about is himself. And he's like, "Hey, bitch, if you think I'm gonna give you everything I worked for all my life, you're crazy."

So this is where we're at right now. With them on this divorce battlefield like two armies. And guess who's in between? You got it—Arianna. And it's, like, a no-win situation. I can't be nice to either one, because if the other one finds out, I get static big time. So I have to stand back neutral while they go at each other like junkyard dogs.

23

My mom has this lawyer who was recommended by her best friend, Rita. He handled Rita's divorce and got everything the old man, had right down to his shorts. My dad's guy is this overstuffed jerk in pinstripe suits and two-tone shoes who looks like Harvard and talks like a used-car salesman. They're both total fools.

Yesterday Mom gets this letter from Mr. Pinstripe asking for an audit of her income, her tax statements, and other personal and financial stuff. She goes ballistic, throwing stuff, using language you wouldn't believe.

Then, when Dad comes by late last night to pick up some old sporting-goods stuff, they get into it right in the driveway and you can hear them all the way to Moscow. Neighbors' lights are going on like flashbulbs and people are peeking out their windows like in a spy movie. You talk about embarrassing, man.

I sure hope they get everything settled before long, get all the money problems ironed out. Not that there's gonna be a whole lot left with legal beagles whacking 'em at four hundred bucks an hour.

And they wonder why kids wanna live together rather than get married. Wow!

FRAN

Fran, through an anonymous letter after her biological mother's death, has discovered that she was adopted. In this speech, she expresses bitterness for her sense of loss, betrayal, and feelings of abandonment.

(*sobbs, letter in hand*) Why didn't you tell me? Why the hell didn't you tell me? (*shakes letter*) If I hadn't gotten this anonymous letter, I'd never have known. I'd have just gone on thinking you were my real parents. How the hell could you do this to me? And now I find out my real mother is dead. And all because of you, you lying, deceitful bitch! (*beat*) Don't tell me that. Get away from me. You don't give a damn about me. Don't touch me. If you really cared anything about me, you would've told me years ago, and I could have found my real mother and known her and known stuff about my past. Now it's over, the door is closed.

Do you have any idea how I feel right now? You have any idea? (*beat*) The hell you do. How can you? You have your mother and father, you know who they are, you have a past. Me—nothing. No past, no future. All I have to look forward to is a trip down to Springfield and a funeral home where there's a body in a casket that was once a living thing that carried me inside her. The first time I see my real mother she'll be dead.

I hate you! And I hate the person who's pretended to be my father all these years. My real father? (*shakes letter*) According to this nice little piece of paper, I was a bastard, because she didn't know who the father was. And I hate her, too. Hate her for being an irresponsible slut. But more than that, I hate her for for giving me up, for handing me over like a loaf of bread. And I'll never forgive her for not coming forward, for not trying to get in touch with me all these years—her own daughter. This is the worst part. How can you walk away from your child just like that?

   And you! Keeping it a secret, keeping if from me, letting me grow up as part of a lie. How could you? How? (*beat*) Because you were afraid of losing me? This is your reason? Good God! It would have been just the opposite, it would have been a way of keeping me. If you'd only told the truth.

   But now, by covering up, you lose.

   Everybody does.

NAOMI

So far as Naomi is concerned, her relationship with Jimmy is grounded in mutual interests. She suspects, however, that for him it's much more. Here, she tactfully sets him straight on the issue.

Now, look. We gotta get straight what's going on here, okay? When we first met in theater and liked the same plays and same movies and stuff, this was cool. I mean, I was really happy I'd found someone who was into my way of thinking, into the same old movies and stars of the thirties and stuff. It's great to be able to relate, you know. And, like, I really appreciate you taping movies for me and cutting basketball and track to tutor me with my math. But it seems, like, seems as though maybe I'm not getting a clear picture here.

Ya know, Jim, it's, like, I've always thought of us as just good buds, you know. Just good buds who're into the same stuff, enjoy the same stuff and like that, you know? And this is all okay. This is really neat. It's not very often you meet someone who likes to watch old Fred Astaire movies. Most of my friends think I'm lame for this. But lately, lately I'm starting to get the impression that you either think our relationship is a lot more than it really is, or that you want it to become a lot more.

What I'm trying to say here is that maybe you really don't like all the stuff I do as much as you let on. That maybe you're just pretending because it's a way of, like, well . . . dating. (*beat*) Okay, okay. Like don't get crazy, okay? Calm down, all right?

Remember when we did that scene together? The one I picked from *Our Town?* I think you got the wrong impression

27

from that; I think you took it as a real-life thing between you and me. Because it was kinda romantic, I mean. (*beat*) Well, maybe not, but after that your attitude toward me changed and you started treating me like we were way married, or something. (*beat*) But you did. And you still do, Jimmy. (*beat*) Yes, you do.

At first I didn't see it. But when my friends mentioned it, it opened my eyes. They clued me. I mean, after all, they were outside looking in, able to see the thing more clearly.

What I'm getting at here is, if you're just pretending to like the stuff I do to get next to me in more than just a friendship thing, it won't happen, okay? Even though I really like you and enjoy your company and that, it's nothing more than this. The thing between us is nothing more than, like, this friendship because of mutual interests. I want you to understand this now so you won't be expecting more.

You're really a super-neat person, Jimmy. I just want you to understand that this isn't *Our Town,* this is real life.

JOYCE

Taking your driver's test may be anxiet- ridden, but what lies beyond can often be more troublesome.

It's easy to ace your driver's written test. Nothing to it. All you have to do is memorize all of this crap about speed laws and signs and how to make a left turn and stuff. Like making a left turn is this big deal, right? Duh. To make a left turn, you turn left. Everything you need to know about driving is in this cheap little booklet with stupid cartoons like my idiot brother draws. You'd think the state could afford better. Anyway, memorizing the book is nothing. It's the actual driver's exam that gets me uptight.

Of course I have to get this examiner who has no sense of humor whatsoever. And he's big. Like ten feet eleven. Was like riding next to the World Trade Center. And he's super grouchy. He's like, "Turn left. Turn right. Look over your shoulder. Move over to the center. Stop." "Please" is not a word in this man's vocabulary. Hey, you're nervous enough already without some sweaty gorilla in dirty jeans barking at you like you're low-mental. And he had bad breath, too. And it was cold, so I couldn't put down the window. Was like riding around in a garbage truck. Try not inhaling for fifteen minutes.

When he asked me to park, I freaked. My friends never had to park, so I just figured I was cool. But this mountain of halitosis asks me to park. Hey, I don't know how I ever did it. Just luck, I guess. Whipped right into the space on the first try. Good thing he didn't see that my eyes were closed.

After we get back, we pull into the parking lot, where the nerd sits going over his checklist. He's making these little marks and circles and is like "Hum, ah, hum," under his breath. I was

29

certain I flunked. I had this vision of walking everywhere for the rest of my life. (*shudders at the thought*)

After what seems like forever, he goes, "You passed." Wow. I couldn't believe it. Man, was I ever relieved. Guess the goon wasn't such a goon after all.

So now I've got my license and I'm gonna be on wheels in our new SUV. Everything's cool except for one thing: I have to pay for my own insurance, which is out of sight because teens have this habit of crashing into stuff while changing CDs. So I took a job at Burger King in order to pay the stupid insurance premium.

Know what? I found out that there's something a whole lot worse than taking your driver's test. It's called WORKING!

YOUNG MEN

JOSH

*There must be something worse than going on Spring Break
with your mother and sisters, but not to hear Josh tell it.*

Wanna get totally bummed? Go on Spring Break with you mom
and sisters. Wow. The rotten worst. The bottom, man. Hanging
out for a week at some cheap motel, crammed into two rooms
with a bunch of women—forget it. This is what I just got set
free from, from two weeks with three women with voices like
bad brakes. Two weeks of wet bras and pantyhose smacking
you in the face when you take a shower, two weeks of bitching
and complaining and stupid giggling and daytime TV—soaps. It
was the vacation from hell.

I tried to get out of it, to stay home, but they wouldn't hear
of it because my old man was gonna be out of town and they
didn't think it was a good idea for me to be home alone. I
begged, I pleaded, I even faked being sick. Didn't work. I had to
go along on this stupid damned female safari because, *(miming
high-pitched, whining voices)* "Little Joshy couldn't stay home
all by his little self, he'd be lonesome, he wouldn't get enough
to eat". *(normal voice)* And, of course, my sisters put up this big
thing about wanting me to come along. BS. They were pissed at
the thought of me being totally free while they're holed up in
some yesterday's rat trap. Women. This was what was behind it.
This and that my jerk sisters have more acne than brains.

So we rent these motel rooms is a place that looks like 1960.
No way the place is in the Auto Club books. This was "X-Files"
time. Weird. And the place is two blocks off the main drag
where the action is and next to a body shop where guys are
testing their hammers ten hours a day. And I gotta share a room
with Doris, who spends most of her time popping her gum and

33

checking out pre-teen boobs that look like golf balls. And then I gotta hear all this silly talk about rock stars and movie stars and cute clothes and cool shoes and neat hair. I never realized what a big thing hair is. Even my mom, she's big into hair, too. Hair is it. Hair rules. Hair is everything, the most important, hair comes first. Hair—then the Salk vaccine. So this is what I'm hearing from morning to night—breakfast, lunch, and dinner. Even by the cheesy pool with the torn vinyl lounges and old women rubbing oil on their varicose veins I gotta hear about hair. For a week. A week!

Next year I'm breaking a leg.

KIP

Kip and Ron have been driving around in circles for hours trying to find Ron's grandparents' farm. In this scene, they have once again pulled to the side of the road to consult the map. And Kip's patience is history. He's fed up with Ron's miscalculations, misdirections, and general sense of disorientation.

Bull! We don't turn right, we turn left! We turn right we wind up in Dingleville, Ratfield, Barfwood—whatever. We turn left, I'm telling you. (*beat*) Hey, man, like we've been following your directions for hours and we're getting, like, nowhere, we're just driving around in circles. And now we're really lost. Look around. Check it out. We're in the middle of Diddleflats. Take a good look around, man. I'm like, this is a scene from *Deliverance,* okay? Only difference is, the pinhead here is behind the wheel and instead of playing "Dueling Banjoes", we're playing "Dueling Road Maps". At this rate, we're never gonna get to your grandparents' place. And I don't wanna get caught out here at night. This place is way *weird.* (*beat*) Okay, okay, show me on the map. (*beat*) No way. Forget it. We aren't there (*stabbing finger to map*), we're somewhere around here. Where the hell ever "here" is.

And going and asking that farmer for directions. You think that nerd knew? He probably hasn't been more than a mile from his house in twenty years. You get a good look at 'im? Really good. Spaced. Vacant. Nothing upstairs. Rooms for rent. When I looked in his eyes I could see the back of his head. And you go and follow his directions like the guy's an astronaut, or something. And now look where we are: on a narrow dirt road that's getting narrower, not a house in sight, haven't passed a

car in a half-hour,and in twenty minutes it's gonna be dark.
(*beat*)

You think it's around here somewhere. Great. You think.
You *don't* think, that's the problem. Or maybe this is the
problem, that you're thinking. Don't think! Please, stop
thinking. You're gonna think us into oblivion. A few more
hours of this and we'll vanish from the face of the earth. "What
ever happened to Ron and Kip?," they'll ask. "Last we heard,
they were somewhere in the middle of Kentucky. Maybe they
were taken for revenuers."

Hey, I never though of that. What if a bunch of gap-toothed
moonshiners jump us? We could wind up becoming fertilizer in
some woods someplace. Turn this thing around, fast. I wanna
get outta here, back to civilization.

I'm gonna fall down on my knees at the sight of the first
Burger King.

DAVE

Poor Dave. His mother, ever one for "the new," has fallen for Feng Shui (fung shway), and has also sucked his sister into this ancient Chinese philosophy, resulting in a home of plainness and sterility—which was okay until it affected his personal environment.

My mom is really neat, loving and all that, but she tends to go off the deep end every once in a while. Like with diets and religions and causes, and stuff. For instance, awhile back she got into this off-the-wall religion that's kinda, like, God for Everyman: no guilt, no hell, no problems—except you had to go every week and were expected to donate, like, lots of bread. When she found out she was supposed to give twemty percent of her salary, she got unreligious super fast.

Her latest bit was this ancient Chinese thing Feng Shui, which is cool, I guess, if you're an ancient Chinese. The thing is, you gotta get rid of clutter in order to find your way to bliss. It's, like, this mystic way to enlightenment through decorating. Hey! Didn't I say she went off the deep end?

Okay, so one night she comes home from this adult-education class full of screwy junk about how putting order in our home would result in us feeling more energized and grounded and balanced—all kinds of far-out crap. Like we gotta paint our front door red, fill in dead zones, get rid of clutter, and rearrange the furniture as a means of tapping into our house's energy. My sister ate it up. To me it sounded like the totally dumb BS you read in *Star* magazine.

Next day I come home from school and find the place looking like the county morgue. No magazines, no papers, nothing on the walls, coffee tables, desk—nothing. And the furniture had been totally rearranged. For a couple of seconds I thought I was in the wrong house.

Then, when I go into my bedroom, I'm like, What the hell's going on here! It was like walking into an army barracks. My bed's backwards, all my posters are gone, pennants down, no rug on the floor, no books, nothing anywhere in sight. I was like naked. And this is bliss?

When I go to my sisters' room, I see she's still got her fan mags, and on my mom's dresser there's still this collection of cosmetics. I guess Feng Shui is just for guys. I spin out, man. I grab up the magazines and cosmetics and dump them in the trash. Now Darlene and mom were Feng Shui, too.

When they come home and can't find their stuff, I tell 'em I've dumped it because it was getting in the way of my spirituality and wisdom and serenity and that I couldn't have it around.

That did it. That was the end of Feng Shui. We've all agreed that it's more enlightening living like pigs.

JOHN

John lives academically in the shadow of brother Jerry who has become an unbearable know-it-all. Here he brings Jerry up to speed regarding his behavior and the ultimate realities of remaining an insufferable, put-down snob.

Yeah, well, it's always been easy for you. For me it's major stuff, okay. You come home with straight-As, I'm afraid to show up because the folks will do a number on me for not coming up to your standards. (*beat*) Oh, really? Well, bro, this is how I'm judged, by Jerry, my genius, super-smart, Mr. Everything brother, Mr. Number One in the brains department. You know what kind pf pressure this put me under, man? You ever stop to think how living in your shadow affects my life? Not that I have anything against your being smart, it's just the way you come on with it, man. Like a real smart-ass know-it-all. (*beat*) Oh, you don't, huh? Hey, how come you don't have any friends, how come they've all split? Ever think about this? How come when you walk down the halls people get out of the way like you got smallpox, or something?

Why you think Jean dumped you for Earl Kramer, a beanpole dork underachiever with space glasses and Banlon shirts? Because you've became an obnoxious jerk, that's why; running around spouting a bunch of intellectual crap all the time, quoting Shakespeare and criticizing everything. Kramer may be, like, duh, but he's got it all over you in the nice department.

It's, like, you've become too good for everyone—especially me. And I'm up to here with it, man. Especially the way you talk down to me and make me look bad in front of Mom and Dad all the time. What the hell you get out of this, anyway, some kind of cheap thrill for being Mr. Up-the-Butt with knowledge?

If this is what smarts is all about, I'll stay with being an average, everyday person with more on his mind than the date Beethoven went deaf and a whole lot of other silly garbage that nobody in their right mind wants to know about.

Know what, Jer? You've become a class-A fool. (*beat*) Oh, yeah! Don't think about it. Unless you also know a lot about home dentistry.

You better wise up, man, before you're hated by everybody. Turn some of that super-intellect into some common sense. And remember, Einstein, the next time you pull your stuff on me in front of Mom and Dad, you're gonna get a Master's Degree in black-and-blue.

DANNY

The community is up in arms because a teacher of fourteen years has revealed his homosexuality. In this speech, Danny defends the man and appeals to a friend for support and understanding.

Like he never did anything to me, okay? Like he was always straight up and down, no problems. (*beat*) C'mon, how you know that? You don't. You're just repeating what you hear around school and what your parents say, and like that. What about *your* opinion, huh? What about what *you* think? (*beat*) BS, man, you're just repeating the buzz, the stupid, off-the-wall buzz that's floating around.

And, besides, what the hell difference does it make? He's one hell of a good teacher, the only teacher in this place who doesn't get me into a giant head bob. In Pearson's class I stay awake because the guy has something to say, man, something to pass on, something he gets across because he makes history interesting, makes it live. So what the hell does him being gay have to do with anything? (*beat*) Aw, man. Like him being gay is gonna rub off on you, or something. Like this is really stupid.

Pearson's been teaching here for over fourteen years and now, because he came out, everybody's all, "Wow! Gay! What a terrible guy. Better lock up the kids in the cellar so's the big bad gay man won't get 'em." Double BS crap! Alluva sudden now, overnight, the guy's different. Hell, he's always been gay! And before anyone knew it, he was Mr. Fantastic Wonderful Educator, picked as the teacher of the year four years in a row. Now, overnight, the dude's garbage.

Ask yourself, man, get inside your head, *think!* Don't go listening to a bunch of screwed-up, prejudiced fools who are so full of fear they're dangerous.

Look, what we got here is people behaving without thinking because they're thinking with their emotions and prejudices, and because of this, they're about to kick out a guy who's a neat person and one helluva great teacher, a guy who's gone the extra mile for a lot of us and a whole bunch of kids over the years. Fourteen years he's been the best, and he's still the best. I'll take one of him gay to fifty of these boring, insensitive bastards who don't teach squat. Pearson's cool, and he needs our help now, our support. We gotta speak up for him, stand up and be real. Lemme ask you, who stayed late with you, after hours, helping you? Who's responsible for you getting a passing grade? Pearson, man, Pearson. So you can't go letting him down.

We don't stand up for what's right now, what kinda adults we gonna make? (*beat*) Good. All right! (*hign five*) That's what I wanted to hear.

RALPH

At his parents' insistence, Ralph has taken a job that is not to his liking. The hours suck, the environment is polluted, and his hands are a mess. Here, he complains to his buddy:

Like they kept after me, you know. Like they kept hounding me, "You gotta get a part-time job if you wanna drive because we're not paying for the car insurance." And, like, my old man's this VP with a hundred people working for him who makes more bread than the local bakery. But I gotta work because he did when he was a kid because he was poor and underprivileged and lived in a shack on the outskirts of Detroit. It's the old Abe Lincoln thing with walking to school through ten feet of snow in zero weather and doing your homework by firelight on the back of a shovel. Hey, who knows this for sure? I hate the Abe Lincoln thing. I think it's a crock. He was probably like this regular lazy kid with poor grades and his mind on babes and a horse and buggy instead of a BMW. "Four score and seven beers ago . . . " Know what I mean?

They were on my back constantly. "Working'll make a man outta you." "The responsibility will be good for you." "You gotta learn about money." Hell, I know about money. It's the green paper stuff that you never get enough of.

They're after me day and night. So, finally, I realize if I'm ever gonna have wheels, I gotta get a job.

You know this shop, the one in the alley behind Sears, the one that looks like 1920? (*beat*) Yeah, that one. Well, they have this sign on the door that says, "Help Wanted." So, I figure, what the hell. So I go in. The place is dark and smells like a bad transmission. This guy comes over and we talk and he hires me

43

to sort parts. My hours are from three to five Monday through Friday and eight till noon on Saturday.

I been working for three weeks. Separating hot, greasy, steel parts and tossing 'em in crates. A real no-brainer. And boring. Monkey work. And depressing because the place is, like, dark because there aren't any windows. The people who work there never see the light of day. Sometime I get the feeling I'm working with a bunch of vampires.

And get a load of my hands, man. Dig. Enough grease to lube your Chevy. And you can't get it out, it's more or less permanent. So what's the diff if I can drive or not? No babe's gonna go out with a guy wearing gloves.

Tomorrow I'm outta there. I'm telling 'em to shove it sideways. So I ain't like Abe Lincoln, so what? Besides, who wants to wind up getting shot?

TOBY

Toby, a teen alcoholic, speaks of his problem at an AA meeting.

My name is Toby, and I'm an alcoholic. Both my mom and dad are alcoholics. I started drinking when I was just twelve years old. Beer. I used to clean up after my parents' parties and I'd drink what was left over in some of the bottles. I thought it was cool and it made me feel grown up and I liked the taste. Too much, I guess, because, before I knew it, I was hooked, you know.

It's funny how you get into bad habits. They just kinda sneak up on you. You don't realize, because you're just enjoying yourself and thinking it's okay and that you can stop whenever you want. You're all, "This is okay, this is grownup, this makes me special and cool." Until you try to stop and realize that you can't because you have this craving for alcohol that you can't beat back. You try, but you can't win the battle.

At first beer was my thing. Until I found out I got a better buzz from the hard stuff—whiskey, vodka, gin and stuff. So I got into my parents' stash whenever I could. A lot of mornings, before going to school, I'd sneak down to the liquor cabinet and have a few hits. I'd be buzzed going out the door. Lost of times in class I was totally wasted.

My folks caught on because their booze supply was going fast. I figured they'd never notice because half the time they were bombed themselves; bombed and sloppy and arguing and treating each other like hell. It was, like, total war between them when they were drinking.

They went ballistic. Like they didn't have a problem themselves, okay? They threatened me and yelled a t me. It was a very bad scene. When I told my dad he had no right to yell at

45

me because he was an old drunk, he goes into a rage and smacked me—almost broke my arm. Mom had to get between us.

This is when they decided to get into AA, when they realized how their habit had been passed along to their kid and what kind of family problem it was causing. And I think my dad hitting me really snapped them back. And me, too.

We're all in AA now, and we're all clean, have been for months. It's like a new life for all of us, a whole new family.

Being clean is great. Fantastic. The best way I can explain it is it's like being free from, like, this jail where you were holding yourself prisoner.

Man, it sure is great being on the outside.

DAREN

Daren fails to see Moby Dick *as either an exciting sea story or a heavily symbolic inquiry into good and evil. To him, it's na arcane, overwritten, hard-to-read assignment.*

I don't care if it *is* a masterpiece. So what? I still don't know what it means. (*holding up the book*) Nobody knows what this means, Carole, and anyone who says they do is, like, full of whale blubber. You think this Melville character knew what it meant? No way. Had to be bombed when he wrote it; came home wasted one night on ten pints of brewskie and decided to write off his hangover. So he goes and comes up with this ridiculous thing about some screwed-up,one-legged sailor whose hung up on this big fish. Was this dude married? Bet his old lady hated his guts for wasting his time on this kinda junk when he coulda been out pushing buggy whips. (*beat*)

So it's an allegory, so what? It's still an overwritten piece of crap by some dude who had mental problems, big time. Who else could dream up a far-out guy like this Captain Ahab character? You gotta be whacked to come up with this kinda stuff. Far as I'm concerned, this is nothing but a big, boring waste of paper and my time. The story sucks. Hell, there isn't even a car chase. Know what? I think the fact that Melville got captured by cannibals had a lot to do with it. I mean, when a guy goes day after day not knowing if what's for dinner is him, he's gotta come loose around the edges, you know. (*beat*)

Okay, all right, so I get an F. So, big deal. I ain't about to go reading this whole thing. You kidding, I don't believe in reading books that are too heavy to lift. (*thumbs pages*) Look at the size of this thing. (*beat*) Look, Carole, you can tutor me all you want, but how you expect me to get into some lame garbage about some nut chasing a white whale around the ocean?

(*shakes the book*) It says here in the front of the book that Herman died broke and nobody ever heard of him. No wonder. No laughs. No sex. This thing is depressing, man, and people back in 1850 had enough to worry about without penicillin and TV. (*beat*) No! They made a movie of it? Get out! How could they? And who'd wanna see it, anyway? Only way I can see it as a flick is if they update it with Ahab in outer space chasing an alien white galaxy. Yeah. This would be cool. Otherwise . . . forget about it.

Let's go get a Coke.

DEXTER

A fellow student recently drew a firearm on a teacher. He was a greatly disturbed individual, but people—friends, family, faculty—overlooked the signs of aberrance. But not Dexter, he was hip to the disastrous potentials.

That's big-time BS, man. The dude was always strange. Like spaced, you know. Always. And underweight between the ears. (*beat*) So what, he was an A student? So what? What I'm talking about here hasn't got to do with book smarts, okay? Got nothing to do with ABCs, man. It's, like, I'm talking about reality and the everyday scene. In this area he was very, very light in the IQ. Like dig the way he dressed, and everything: with the black hat and sunglasses and stormtrooper boots. (*beat*) You didn't think this was weird? Know what, Norm, sometimes I think you need to have your oil and filter changed. You nuts, or something? Ralph was a walking disaster, man. What I don't get is why people didn't see it.

"Oh, he's just different, he's just creative," everyone would say. Yeah, creative all right, if you call creative having a swastika tattooed on your arm. The dude was a trouble machine. (*beat*) You couldn't see it. Yeah, I guess nobody else could, either, the other kids, the teachers, his parents, even. They just shined him on as being "different,"

Know what, Norm, you're either naive or just plain stupid. (*beat*) Cool it, okay? Cool it and ease back and don't get pissed because Ralph Merideth snowed you like everyone else; took all of you by surprise when he pulled a gun on Mr. Whitcomb.

This is what too much psychology gets you, what happens when you get yourself all wrapped around psychology instead of facing up to the facts and what's right before your eyes.

Merideth was a nut case from day one. In trouble. Weird. Outside. Up in the counselor's office every week. And the stupid counselor sits there talking Freud to this mental meatloaf. You'd think the tattoo woulda told him something, woulda told him that they needed to drop the net on the weirdo. But noooo, he was just misunderstood, a product of his environment. Hey, apparently his environment was in Germany in 1932.

So don't talk to me about compassion and love and all this other doves-and-roses-up-the-butt nonsense. (*beat*) Willya shut up and listen? What I'm talking about here is signs, man, signs. You gotta be able to read the signs. And on Merideth they were hanging out like billboards. They were saying, "Look at me, people, I'm a ticking time-bomb weirdo psycho." But no one could see it because he was "creative." Lotsa people thought Hitler was creative, too. Yeah. Right. And he wound up creating the planet out of six million Jews.

Quit sleep-walking, man.

LES

What does the new owner of a cell phone do? Why, call everyone, of course.

(*punching in numbers*) Hi, Cindy . . . Not much, just hanging out, you know. How about you? . . . Hey, what you up to? . . . What is it with the hair, anyway, you wash it every hour? . . . Well, it seems like it. Hey, guess what? . . . No, I didn't flunk English. I got me a cell phone . . . Yeah . . . The old man finally broke down. I told him it was way dangerous riding around without a phone these days . . . He's covering the monthly thing and I gotta pick up for the calls . . . Yeah, it's really cool being digital . . . Naw, I'm not makin' a bunch of stupid calls. No way. This phone's for emergencies, man. Besides, I'm not about to be turning into a cell-phone junkie like most people. Most people with cell phones suck, you know . . . Yeah, right, absolutely, like the thing's grafted to their ear. I hate it when they whip it out in a restaurant and you gotta listen to them rapping over nothing right in the middle of your steak, you know. Last week this guy was on his phone in church. In church, man! . . . I'm not kidding. The dude was yelling at his accountant, and you could hear the fool over the choir. Rude, man, really super rude . . . Yeah, right . . . Don't some people make you wanna barf? No class. They got no respect or common sense. Like I said, I'm using this phone for emergencies *only,* like when I'm stuck on the freeway or lost someplace or late, or something. My brother-in-law, Herb, rather than walk fifty feet he cell-phones my sister from the other side of the house. He also has this little case on his belt he keeps his phone in, like this holster so he can whip it out like he's the fastest phone in the West. Sickening. He also has Direct

TV . . . I know. What a turkey. I don't know what my sister sees in him . . . Don't worry about me, I'll never be a cell freak, it's not my conservative nature. Like I said, strictly for emergencies . . . Yeah, I know, but you're different, Cin. I mean, you being my crush puts you right away on an emergency basis. I got you on speed dial. Right after 911. Hey, how bout drying that mop and we go out for burgers? . . . Huh? Whadaya mean, how long will it take me to get there? I'm, like, right out front of your house.

BEN

Only the most naive could believe that Elvis is still on the planet. Just more irresponsible nonsense propagated by rumor, ignorance, and gross superstition. Or . . . ?

We were driving through the South—Mom and Dad, my sister and I—driving through this remote area in southern Alabama. We were about two hours out of Montgomery when we came to this crazy little town. It'd been a while since breakfast, so we decided to stop for lunch.

We go into a local diner and seat ourselves in a ripped-up booth. A few customers were hanging out at the counter, all gathered around this scraggly looking old dude who was gesturing like crazy with this wild look in his eyes.

We waited and waited, but nobody came over to take our order—they were all too busy listening to this old guy with glassy eyes and no teeth. Finally, after my dad yells for service, this woman comes over and gets on our case for interrupting. Says that the old dude had seen Elvis again the night before and was giving them a rundown on the encounter.

We looked at each other, like, I mean, well hey . . . is she kidding? My dad says, "I gotta hear this." So we all ease over to the counter and listen in.

The old dude's going, "I come up over Pengrove Hill 'bout quarter o' seven last evening when I see this here pink Caddy settin' under that big maple near the intersection of 422. We'll, I knew right away it was Elvis again. If you all remember , I seen 'im out there 'bout two weeks back, the same day Merle Johnson seen 'im over near four corners. Well, there 'e was, just as big as ya please, settin' there chewin' on a double cheeseburg. No wonder the boy got s' damned fat.

53

"I git out and go on over. We chit chat 'bout this an' that. He's still pissed about Tom Parker gettin' all them royalties, how the Las Vegas crowd ain't worth sawdust, and how Priscilla's cashin' in on Graceland. Same old stuff. A broken record—excuse the expression. Then he tells me somethin' I ain't never heard before."

At this point everybody leaned in.

"You know how he got away with it, fakin' dying, that is? Well, seems this here Elvis impersonator up in Vegas owned a bunch o' gambling debts and one night he winds up out in the desert with a hole in his sideburn. Well, this guy who worked for the coroner tipped off one of the Jordanaires who tells Elvis, who'e fed up with the night life and the sin and degradation, and they cook up this deal to bury the guy in place of Presley. "

It was quite a story. And these idiots never questioned it. Seems like everybody in town had seen Elvis someplace or other: At the 7-11, the bowling alley, buying Prestone at Wal-Mart. Far out. We couldn't believe people could be so stupid. It cracked us up. We had some burgers and fries and split.

Two miles down the road we were still, like, laughing when this big pink Eldorado blows past like we were in reverse. We couldn't see the driver, but the radio was blaring "Hound Dog."

Don't ask.

CONWAY

Having Cokes with Nicole's arch rival has been blown out of proportion by her friends and her active imagination. Here, Conway sets the record straight.

(*running up to her*) Nicole, Stop! Stop, I gotta talk to you. (*beat*) I just do. (*beat*) Gimme a minute here, willya? I'm going nuts. Look, I know you're pissed, but you can at least gimme a chance here. I got questions, okay? Lotsa questions I gotta get off my chest before I explode. (*beat*) Naw, I'm not phoning. Forget phoning. Besides, you won't answer my calls. I left fifty messages this weekend. (*beat*) BS. You know damned well you got 'em. C'mon. So don't go avoiding me, okay?

Look, I know I goofed, I know what I did was totally uncool, but don't go shutting me out forever because of it. People make mistakes, you know, people mess up because they're people, because they're human. (*beat*) But it wasn't intentional. (*beat*) Because I'm telling you it wasn't, that's why. So gimme a break, okay? Look, it was totally thoughtless and unfeeling, I admit this. But it wasn't a plan. When Jerry mentioned picking up Doris and Ruby, I just went along. And there wasn't anything to it. Where I screwed up was not telling you right away before your little gossip factory, your little, ignorant, trouble-making, so-called "friends" bent the whole thing way outta shape.

(*takes her arm*) Hold on! Don't go. Please! Please, don't go. Look, all we did was stop off for Cokes at Jimmy's, nothing more. (*beat*) So Doris has the hots for me, can I help this? Is this my fault? (*beat*) Say what? No way she's gonna take me away from you, no way! How could you think this? (*long beat*)

Wow, that's huge, Nicole. But why didn't you tell me how you felt a long time ago? I didn't have any idea. Like I know we're a pair and all that, steadies, you know. But I never realized you cared this much. Like you never said anything.

Look, I feel exactly the same way. (*beat*) Yeah, I do. I mean, like, it's way more than just liking you a lot. It's . . . it's way more than this. And if you think I'd go messing us up for some slut like Doris Washburn, you're crazy, girl.

Hey! Look at me here. Look at me.

I *love* you, Nicole.

ANDREW

Andrew's younger brother is a profligate whose acts have brought social disgrace and financial ruin to the family. Here, shortly after their father's funeral, Andrew sets him straight in no uncertain terms.

Don't go giving me this, you little bastard. Don't alluva sudden go telling me how much you loved him. He's been in the ground for no more than an hour and now, alluva sudden, you loved him and respected him. Yeah, sure, you irresponsible little jerk.

You didn't respect him, you disrespected him, treated him like hell, and drove him nuts with your off-the-wall behavior and drugs and drinking. All you were for him was a ten-ton pain in the butt. For him and Mom, too. You've been nothing but problems and heartaches. And now, after he's gone, you loved him and respected him. You got lotsa nerve, bro.

You got any idea what love and respect means? What it really means? It means being responsible and being in control and caring about how your actions affect other people, especially your family and friends. And all this takes balls, man, balls and guts and resisting the easy ways of life. And this ain't you, jerk off! You're the opposite of this; you're all about messing-up and going out of control and laying the blame on others.

You call respect piling up the car? You call taking off for three days with your jerk friends and sending Mom and Dad up the wall with worry respect? You call sassing back respect? You call getting busted for dope respect? You call acting like a big man with a bunch of lowlife degenerates respect?

You don't know the meaning of respect. And you didn't love Dad. Hell, it's no wonder he had a heart attack. If anything, you drove him to it. You damned near broke him with the lawsuit because of the kid you killed when you ran the light down at 5th and Main. It broke him financially and broke his heart. Your damned irresponsibility broke and disgraced the family. And he stood by you. And what did you give back? Sarcasm and arrogance because you're an irresponsible, self-centered, out-of-control fool.

So don't come around me with your sorrow and sadness. Where the hell were you when he was alive, when it counted?

Get lost!

KEN

Ken, wheelchair-bound, describes the fateful date he was shot by a fellow student, the subsequent ordeal, his feelings.

I was getting my books from my locker to go to World Civ when I heard these sounds that sounded like firecrackers. I thought it was a joke at first, until I saw Richard in the hallway with a gun. Then I felt this feeling in my back, like someone had punched me. I knew I'd been shot.

I didn't feel any pain, I just fell to the floor. But I knew I was paralyzed, because I couldn't feel my legs.

Jimmy ran over to me and put his hand under my head and told me to be calm, to be strong. He was the calm one.

I could see Richard shooting and hear kids screaming. A bullet grazed my hair. Then Jimmy was hit. He got it worse than all of us.

I spent the next six months in hospitals. At least I survived. Three of the five of us who were shot didn't make it. At first I felt real guilty about what had happened to Jimmy. But my mom said I shouldn't blame myself for him being so brave.

Now this wheelchair and being paralyzed is my constant reminder of what happened. But maybe there's some reason for it.

They wanted to give me this motorized chair, but I decided on this lightweight one that I have to maneuver because it makes me feel like I'm in control and not such an invalid. I get around pretty good. I go to the mall, the bowling alley, pretty much everywhere. I still have full use of my arms. I can even play basketball in this thing. And I can swim, so I chill out in my neighbor's pool which is neat because I'm away from the wheelchair and can move around.

I can wiggle my toes slightly. Look. (*wiggles his toes*) I'm expecting to come back, but the doctors said I shouldn't expect too much. I don't really care about getting feeling back so much, I just want movement. This is my goal.

Sometimes it isn't easy. I have to admit, I do get pretty depressed. It's real frustrating not to be able to walk and participate in things the way I used to. But I'm not giving up.

I've thought about what happened a lot, about Richard and the terrible thing he did. But as hard as it is, you have to forgive. Holding a grudge won't bring back the kids who died, and it won't help me get better. You have to forgive.

Forgiving gives you closure.